NARRATIVE

OF

FACTS IN THE CASE

OF

Passmore Williamson.

PHILADELPHIA:

Published by The Pennsylvania Anti-Slavery Society,

No. 31 NORTH FIFTH STREET.

MERRIHEW & THOMPSON, PRS., MERCHANT ST., ABOVE FOURTH.

1855.

ISBN-13:
978-1497320482

ISBN-10:
1497320488

Passmore Williamson

PASSMORE WILLIAMSON,

IN MOYAMENSING PRISON FOR ALLEDGED CONTEMPT OF COURT.

Photo

- Title: Passmore Williamson, in Moyamensing Prison for alledged contempt of court / on stone by E[mil] Luders ; lith. of A[ugust] Kollner, Phila.
- Creator(s): Luders, Emil, artist
- Related Names:
    Köllner, Augustus, 1813-1906 , lithographer
- Date Created/Published: [Philadelphia] : Published by Thomas Curtis, printseller, 134 Arch St., Phila., c1855.
- Medium: 1 print on wove paper: lithograph with watercolor (chine colle proof) ; image 55.4 x 38.1 cm.
- Summary: An unusual informal portrait of the secretary of the Pennsylvania Abolition Society, seated in a prison cell. Williamson was sentenced on July 22, 1855, to imprisonment for his "false return" (i.e., evasive testimony) to a writ of habeas corpus issued by Federal District Court judge John Kane. Williamson's testimony related to his part in the freeing of three slaves owned by U.S. minister to Nicaragua John Hill Wheeler in Philadelphia. Williamson's imprisonment gave rise to heated public controversy over the issue of states' rights and the status of slaves traveling through free territory. Kane's action was heavily criticized in the press. Williamson was released from prison on November 3, 1855, after giving a new, slightly modified testimony.
- Reproduction Number: LC-DIG-pga-03940 (digital file from original print) LC-USZC4-12565 (color film copy transparency) LC-USZ62-16949 (b&w film copy neg.)
- Rights Advisory: No known restrictions on publication.
- Call Number: PGA - Luders--Passmore... (C size) [P&P]
- Repository: Library of Congress Prints and Photographs Division Washington, D.C. 20540 USA

Narrative of facts in the case of Passmore Williamson.

CREATED/PUBLISHED
Philadelphia, Pennsylvania anti-slavery society, 1855.

NOTES
The escape of Jane Johnson and two children, slaves of John H. Wheeler, the trial of Williamson and others concerned, and the refusal of state supreme court to issue writ of habeas corpus.

SUBJECTS
Johnson, Jane,
Williamson, Passmore.
Fugitive slaves--Legal status, laws, etc.--United States
Slavery--Legal status of slaves in free states.

MEDIUM
24 p. 18 cm.

CALL NUMBER
E450 .N23

PART OF
African American Pamphlet Collection (Library of Congress)

DIGITAL ID
rbaapc 20000

NARRATIVE.

John H. Wheeler, of North Carolina, the accredited Minister of the United States to Nicaragua, arrived in the city of Philadelphia, on his way from Washington to Nicaragua, on Wednesday the 18th of July, 1855. He brought with him Jane Johnson, a woman whom he had purchased as a slave, some two years before, at Richmond, Virginia, and her two children, both sons, one between 6 and 7, and the other between 11 and 12 years of age. His professed design was to hold them as slaves, not only in the free States of Pennsylvania, New Jersey and New York, but also in the free country of Nicaragua. Lawyer by profession, and Diplomatist by occupation, he must have been fully aware that none of the States named tolerated the existence of slavery for a moment within their limits, excepting in the case of slaves escaping from other States. He seems to have relied for immunity upon the respect inspired by his representative character and upon his personal vigilance in guarding Jane and her children.

Upon his arrival at the Baltimore Railroad Depot, corner of Broad and Prime streets, in this city, he conveyed them to Bloodgood's hotel, near Walnut street wharf, stopping on the way at the house of a relative. During the two and a half hours of their stay at Bloodgood's, he lost sight but once of his companions. Jane's intention to assert her freedom at the earliest opportunity, had been fully formed before starting from the South. She is a remarkably intelligent woman for one wholly without education. When Mr. Wheeler was called to dinner, she feared to move, thinking his eye was upon her. It was well she did so, for in a few minutes he left the dining hall to see whether she was still there; and being satisfied on that point, returned to finish a hasty repast. At this time she spoke to a colored woman who was passing, and told her that she was a slave, and to a colored man she said the same thing, afterwards adding, that she wished to be free. An hour afterwards, William Still, an active member of the Vigilance Committee, and clerk at the Philadelphia Anti-Slavery Office, received a note asking him to come down to Bloodgood's hotel as soon as possible, as there were three slaves there who wanted liberty, and that their master was with them, on his way to New York.

With this note in his hand, Mr. Still called upon the Secretary of the Acting Committee of " The Pennsylvania Society for Promoting the Abolition of Slavery, and *for the Relief of Free Negroes unlawfully held in Bondage*, and for improving the condition of the African Race." This Society, whose objects are sufficiently indicated by its name, was incorporated by Legislative Act in 1789 ; Benjamin Franklin was its first President, and it has ever since been an efficient aid to Freedom in Pennsylvania. Mr. Williamson, the present Secretary, is every way worthy to fill his post. Well educated, intelligent, of active habits and sound judgment, he has long enjoyed the respect and unlimited confidence of a large circle of acquaintances and friends.

Ever active at their important posts, Mr. Williamson and Mr. Still hastened to the hotel. Mr. Williamson, who arrived first, found that the party had gone on board the boat then at the wharf, designing to take the five o'clock Camden and Amboy train for New York.— Thither he followed them, and found Jane and her children seated upon the upper deck. He went up to her and said, " You are the person I am looking for, I presume." Mr. Wheeler, who was sitting on the same bench, three or four feet from her, asked what Mr. Williamson wanted with him. The answer was, " Nothing, my business is entirely with this woman." Amid repeated interruptions from Mr. Wheeler, Mr. Williamson calmly explained to Jane that she was free under the laws of Pennsylvania, and could either go with Mr. Wheeler, or enjoy her freedom by going on shore. The conversation between Williamson, Wheeler, Still and a by-stander, was kept up for several minutes, the same ideas being frequently repeated. A few persons gathered about them to hear. Wheeler begged Jane, in the most hurried and earnest manner, to say that she wanted to go with him to her children in Virginia. She made answer that she wanted to see her children, but she wanted to be free. At last the bell rang, and Mr. Williamson, supposing the boat was about to start, turned to Jane and said, " The time has come when you must act; if you wish to exercise your right of freedom, you will have to come ashore immediately." She looked round at her two children, grasped the hand or arm of the one next her, and attempted to rise from her seat. Wheeler pushed her back, saying, " Now don't go, Jane." She renewed her effort to get up, and did so, with the aid of Mr. Williamson. Wheeler's first movement had been to push Jane back, but he soon clasped her tightly round the body. Mr. Williamson pulled him back and held him till she was out of danger from his grasp. Jane moved steadily forward towards the stairway leading to the lower deck. It was at the head of the stairway, if we may believe Mr. Wheeler, that he was seized by two colored men and threatened by one of them ; but the most careful and repeated examination of witnesses has failed to elicit any testimony to a threat except one made on the lower deck. She was led down the stairs of the boat and her children picked up and carried after her ; one of them cried vociferously. She and her children were conducted ashore, and put into a carriage, and, amid the huzzas of the spectators, were driven off to a place of safety. There was a crowd of persons, including some police officers, on and about the boat at the time, but no one offered any resistance. All seemed to regard it as a work proper to be done, and to approve of the manner in which it was executed. Mr. Williamson behaved very judiciously in the affair, and discharged the duty imposed on him, by his office, in a manner becoming its importance. To the threats of Mr. Wheeler, he replied by giving him his card, indicating where he was to be found, if wanted, and saying that he would be responsible for the legal consequences of his action.

In order to judge respecting the legal consequences or character of Passmore Williamson's action in this case, it is necessary to recall certain facts in the legislation of Pennsylvania. On the 1st of March, 1780, the Legislature of Pennsylvania passed an Act providing for the gradual abolition of Slavery within the State.

The following is the Preamble of that Act :

" When we contemplate our abhorrence of that condition to which the arms and tyranny of Great Britain were exerted to reduce us, when we look back on the variety of dangers to which we have been exposed, and how miraculously our wants in many instances have been supplied, and our deliverances wrought, when even hope and human fortitude have become unequal to the conflict, we are unavoidably led to a serious and grateful sense of the manifold blessings, which we have undeservedly received from the hand of that Being, from whom every good and perfect gift cometh. Impressed with these ideas, we conceive that it is our duty, and we rejoice that it is in our power, to extend a portion of that freedom to others which hath been extended to us, and release them from that state of thraldrom to which we ourselves were tyranically doomed, and from which we have now every prospect of being delivered. It is not for us to enquire why, in the creation of mankind, the inhabitants of the several parts of the earth were distinguished by the difference in feature or complexion. It is sufficient to know that all are the work of an Almighty Hand. We find, in the distribution of the human species, that the most fertile as well as the most barren parts of the earth are inhabited by men of complexions different from ours, and from each other; from whence we may reasonably, as well as religiously, infer, that He who placed them in their various situations, hath extended equally his care and protection to all, and that it becometh not us to counteract his mercies. We esteem it a peculiar blessing granted to us, that we are enabled this day to add one more step to universal civilization, by removing, as much as possible, the sorrows of those who have lived in undeserved bondage, and from which, by the assumed authority of the Kings of Great Britain, no effectual legal relief could be obtained. Weaned by a long course of experience from those narrow prejudices and partialities we had imbibed, we find our hearts enlarged with kindness and benevolence towards men of all conditions and nations; and we conceive ourselves at this particular period extraordinarily called upon by the blessings which we have received, to manifest the sincerity of our profession, and to give a substantial proof of our gratitude.

"II. And whereas, the condition of those persons who have heretofore been denominated Negro and Mulatto slaves, has been attended with circumstances, which not only deprived them of the common blessing that they were by nature entitled to, but has cast them into the deepest afflictions by an unnatural separation and sale of husband and wife from each other and from their children, an injury, the greatness of which can only be conceived by supposing that we were in the same unhappy case. In justice, therefore, to persons so unhappily circumstanced, and who, having no prospect before them whereon they may rest their sorrows and their hopes, have no reasonable inducement to render their services to society, which they otherwise might, and also in grateful commemoration of our own happy deliverance from that state of unconditional submission to which we were doomed by the tyranny of Britain:

"III. Be it enacted, and it is hereby enacted," &c.

This Act declares that "no man or woman of any nation or color," (excepting the slaves then living in the State and registered as required by law,) "shall at any time hereafter be deemed, adjudged or holden, within the territories of this commonwealth, as slaves or servants for life, but as free men and free women, except the domestic slaves attending upon delegates in Congress from the other American States, foreign ministers and consuls, and persons passing through and sojourning in this State, and not becoming residents therein, and seamen employed in ships not belonging to any inhabitant of this State, nor employed in any ship owned by any such inhabitant : *Provided*, Such domestic slaves shall not be alienated nor sold to any inhabitant, nor (except in the case of members of Congress, foreign ministers and consuls) retained in this State longer than six months."

On the 3d of March, 1847, the Legislature of Pennsylvania passed a statute, repealing this permission to hold slaves even temporarily in this State. The language of the statute is as follows :

"So much of the Act of the General Assembly, entitled ' An Act for the gradual abolition of Slavery,' passed the 1st day of March, 1780, as authorizes the masters or owners of slaves to bring or retain such slaves within this commonwealth, for the period of six months, in involuntary servitude, or for any period of time whatsoever, and so much of said act as prevents a slave from giving testimony against any person whatsoever, be and the same is hereby repealed."

Thus was freedom established as the rule for the Courts, absolute and unlimited, in all cases of slaves brought into the State by their owners.

The Pennsylvania law on this subject is given with great clearness in 1849, by the Supreme Court, in *Kauffman vs. Oliver*, 10 Barr's Reports:

"The principle sprung fresh, and beautiful, and perfect from the mind of Lord Mansfield, in the great case of the negro Somerset, that, by the common law, a slave, of whatever country or color, the moment he was on English ground, became free—endowed with the sanctity of reason. This case was decided before the revolution, and became the common law of this State, always saving and excepting the inroad of the compact and compromise. This action, then, professes to be founded on the principles of the common law ; but by the principles of law, the fugitives *were free the moment when they touched the soil of Pennsylvania*. All the incidents, accompaniments and attributes of bondage fell from around them."

Immediately after he had been left by his travelling companions Mr. Wheeler sought the potential assistance of John K. Kane, Judge of the District Court of the United States. It seems to have been decided by these gentlemen that a warrant, under the Fugitive Slave Act, could not be sustained—that warrant applying only to cases of slaves escaping from another State into Pennsylvania. The ingenious device was hit upon of making the writ of Habeas Corpus—that

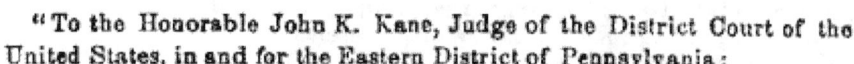

glorious old bulwark of personal liberty—an instrument for getting possession of the mother and her children. Mr. Wheeler made the following affidavit :—

"To the Honorable John K. Kane, Judge of the District Court of the United States, in and for the Eastern District of Pennsylvania:

"The petition of John H. Wheeler respectfully represents :

"That your petitioner is *the owner of three persons* held to labor by the laws of the State of Virginia, said persons being respectively named Jane, aged about 35 years, Daniel, aged about 12 years, and Isaiah, aged about 7 years, persons of color; and that they are detained from the possession of your petitioner by one Passmore Williamson, resident of the city of Philadelphia, and that they are not detained for any criminal or supposed criminal matter.

"Your petitioner therefore prays your Honor to grant a writ of habeas corpus to be directed to the said Passmore Williamson, commanding him to bring before your Honor the bodies of the said Jane, Daniel and Isaiah, to do and abide such order as your Honor may direct.

      [Signed]   JOHN H. WHEELER."

"Sworn to and subscribed, July 18, 1855.

                CHAS. F. HEAZLITT, U. S. Com."

It will be observed that the benefit of the writ is not solicited in behalf of Jane and her children ; Mr. Wheeler does not allege that they are his wife, children, or wards, but that they are slaves ; he does not bring the case within the Fugitive Slave Act, by asserting their escape from another State into Pennsylvania, but rests his claim upon the naked fact that they are his slaves by Virginia law. Instead of promptly rejecting this application, on the ground of want of jurisdiction, Judge Kane granted the writ, returnable on the 18th instant, the next day, at 3 o'clock. All the facts—the sudden departure of Jane, the visit of Mr. Wheeler to Judge Kane, the affidavit, the application, the granting and issuing of the writ—seem to have been crowded into an incredibly short space of time after five o'clock P. M. on the 18th. On the 19th, a Deputy Marshal made affidavit that he had served the writ at the residence of Passmore Williamson. This was a mistake, as he had served it at the residence of his father, corner of Seventh and Arch streets. On its discovery the affidavit was changed in accordance with the fact. An alias writ was issued, returnable at 10 o'clock, A. M. on the 20th.

Mr. Williamson, though under no legal obligation to obey or to notice a writ thus illegally issued, made the following return :

" To the Honorable J. K. Kane, the Judge within named :

Passmore Williamson, the defendant in the within writ mentioned, for return thereto respectfully submits, that the within named Jane, Daniel, and Isaiah, or by whatsoever names they may be called, nor either of them, are not now, nor were at the time of issuing the said writ, or the original writ, *or at any other time*, in the custody, power, or possession of, nor confined, nor restrained their liberty by him, the said Passmore Williamson. Therefore he cannot have the bodies of the said Jane, Daniel and Isaiah, or either of them, before your Honor, as by the said writ he is commanded. (Signed,)

P. WILLIAMSON.

The above named Passmore Williamson, being duly affirmed, says that the facts set forth in the above return are true.
(Signed,) P. WILLIAMSON.

Affirmed and subscribed before me, this 20th day of July, A. D., 1855.
(Signed,) CHAS. F. HEAZLETT,
U. S. Commissioner."

The return is in the ordinary form, with the addition of the words in italics.

Mr. Vandyke, the United States District Attorney and counsel for Mr. Wheeler, objected to the return as insufficient and untrue. Mr. Williamson's counsel contended that the return was complete, that it was not competent to go behind it, and that if the charge of untruth were brought, it should be made the subject of another hearing and of a separate and substantial allegation. Judge Kane said that the testimony offered by Mr. Vandyke should be admitted, and might be such as to make out a prima facie case of perjury, in which event it might be his duty as committing magistrate to bind Passmore Williamson over for perjury. This revelation of the feelings of the Judge changed in a moment the whole aspect of the case. The Judge had become the prosecutor, and before hearing evidence had allowed his feelings to betray him into a violation of the decency of the Bench, and an outrage upon the personal character of one of the most respectable of our citizens.

Mr. W.'s counsel asked for time to examine the case and prepare a proper defense, which was refused by Judge Kane, unless the persons named in the writ were brought into Court. Mr. Vandyke moved for an attachment against Passmore Williamson for contempt, and that he be held to answer a charge of perjury. Mr. W., took the stand, and, under affirmation, made a full and clear statement of the whole transaction, so far as his knowledge of it, and connection with it, extended. His counsel, at the opening, stated that they rested their case upon the fact of entire negation of possession, and were

1*

ready to amend the return in any manner directed by the Court, compatible with that position. But at this stage of the proceedings, they declined an argument, submitting the case to the judgment of the Court. Judge Kane said that in view of the gravity of the case, he would take time to consider it, and in the mean time, the respondent must enter bail, in the sum of $5000, for his appearance on Friday morning, the 27th of July, to answer the charge of perjury; that the motion in relation to contempt would go over till that day, when he would deliver his written opinion on the whole subject. He added, that "he would also say, at the risk of being considered extra judicial, that if it is really in the power of the defendant to produce the bodies of the three persons, it would be better for him to do so," thus leaving little room to doubt that his foregone determination had been to obtain Jane and her children, for the purpose of their re-enslavement, or, failing to do that, to inflict vengeance on the man who had enabled them to assert their legal rights.

These proceedings occupied little time. Nothing further was done until the morning of the 27th, when the Judge took his seat upon the Bench, and, to the surprise of the counsel, abandoned the charge of perjury, and committed the prisoner for contempt. Probably, during the week in which he considered the case, visions of a jury came between him and the man whom he would willingly condemn for perjury, and therefore he chose to construct a case where this troublesome element of American jurisprudence would not interfere with his plans. And thus was an innocent citizen sentenced to indefinite imprisonment, without a hearing, without a trial, without the verdict of a jury of his peers, after having been brow-beaten and charged with crime of a deep dye, by a Judge who should have presumed him innocent until he was proved guilty.

The decision delivered by Judge Kane on this occasion is perhaps the most remarkable legal document of our times. It will certainly be regarded as a barbarism of the nineteenth century, should it be preserved for the criticism of a wiser and better generation. Among its monstrous features it is difficult to decide whether it is most strongly marked by its perversion of the facts, its quibbling ingenuity on the question of constructive custody, or the arrogance with which it nullifies the statute law of Pennsylvania. It is wholly based on a double falsehood, viz: that Jane Johnson did not desire her freedom and was forcibly abducted by Passmore Williamson. It asserts facts in contradiction to the plainest testimony of respectable witnesses, and even contradicts the statement of the Judge's friend,

Mr. Wheeler. It represents Passmore Williamson as heading a riotous mob, the object of which was "*to effect the abduction and imprisonment*" of unoffending citizens. It insists that Jane Johnson and her children were within his custody and control because he told the woman that she was free by Pennsylvania law, and offered to lead her off the boat if she desired to go.

Not the least remarkable passage in this strange document is the following:

"The cause was submitted to me by the learned counsel for the respondent without argument, and I have therefore found myself at some loss to understand the grounds on which, if there be any such, they would claim the discharge of their client."

The reader who recollects that Judge Kane *refused to allow the counsel time for preparation for the argument*, though he took a week to prepare his decision, will not hesitate to characterize this statement as an insult to Mr. Williamson and to his counsel.

Another striking point is the profession of ignorance, on the part of its author, respecting Pennsylvania law. He says that he knows "of no statute of Pennsylvania which affects to divest the right of property of a citizen of North Carolina, acquired and asserted under the laws of that State, because he had found it needful or convenient to pass through the territory of Pennsylvania." By this circumlocution he means that he knows of no law in force in Pennsylvania which would deprive a slaveholder of his power to hold his slaves on her soil, after he had voluntarily brought them hither on his passage to another place. If this is not his meaning, his remark is irrelevant to his argument. Such a defence of his course is, certainly, made at an expense of his reputation for legal knowledge which one would scarcely have expected in a lawyer and judge. Yet, in the very next sentence, he incautiously permits the truth to appear that, after all, he has some idea of the existence of such a law, by expressing his doubt of its recognized validity by a United States' Court. What is this but an insult to Pennsylvania,—an intimation that, as a sovereign State, she has no right to determine whether or not slavery shall be transplanted by Southern masters to her own soil, and the laws of Virginia be dominant here. Again, this law-defying Judge says that he waives the inquiry whether, for the purposes of this question, they (Jane Johnson and her children) were in the territorial jurisdiction of Pennsylvania, while passing from one State to another, upon the navigable waters of the United States;" but adds, that his first impressions, upon this point, are adverse to the argument. One might fairly infer from this clause that Judge Kane had not the slightest idea that these persons had ever set foot on Pennsylvania soil; notwithstanding Wheeler's statement before the Court, that they spent some hours at Bloodgood's Hotel, in Walnut street, and notwithstanding the fact, well known to the Judge, that their route from Washington to New York lay through the heart of the City of Philadelphia. And the utterer of these contemptible quibbles dares to charge Passmore Williamson with falsehood and evasion, and to read to his auditors a homily on the importance of speaking " full, direct, and unequivocal " truth.   After the decision was pronounced, Mr. Williamson's counsel, Hon. Charles Gilpin, rose and addressed the Court in some remarks preliminary to a motion which he intended to make. He had contended that Williamson had not possession or custody of the persons whom he was commanded to produce, and he now suggested that the return should be amended to express this, in a manner conformatory to the views of the Court.   *While he was speaking,* Mr. Vandyke rose and moved that a commitment, under the seal of the Court, be issued, and the defendant, Passmore Williamson, be placed in the custody of the Marshal.   Mr. Gilpin proceeded, when Judge Kane remarked that the District Attorney had precedence, and that any motion of defendant's counsel must be reduced to writing.   Mr. Gilpin was about to reply to the motion of the District Attorney, saying that it had not been reduced to writing, when the Judge announced that it had been already granted.   Such conduct on the part of a judicial officer needs no comment.

While these scenes, so disgraceful to Pennsylvania, were transpiring in the city of Philadelphia, another plot of the minions of slavery was in process of execution.   On the 19th of July, Mr. Wheeler entered complaint before James B. Freeman, Alderman, who issued a warrant for the arrest of Isaiah Moore, Wm. Custis, John Ballard, James Martin, and James S. Braddock, (colored men.) They were arrested and thrown into the "lock up" of a stationhouse, where they were left until the afternoon of the next day, suffering from *intense heat,* without food, and without permission to see their friends.   They were then brought before the magistrate, exhausted with fatigue, want of sleep, excitement and hunger, and held to bail in the excessive sum of $7000 each, to answer to the charges of highway robbery! inciting to riot! riot! and assault and battery.   In default of bail, they were committed to prison.

Passmore Williamson was also arrested on the last three charges.

He had a hearing before Alderman Freeman, and was held to answer in the sum of $6000.

On the 28th of July, Isaiah Moore, Wm. Custis, John Ballard, James Martin, and James S. Braddock were brought before Judge Kelley, on a writ of habeas corpus, and an application made for reduction of bail. Mr. Wheeler was again present, and testified against them. District Attorney Mann abandoned at once the charge of highway robbery, characterizing it as "absurd," and again as "ridiculous." Judge Kelley, after inflicting a reprimand upon the Alderman, reduced the bail to $1000, in the cases of Ballard and Custis, and $500 in the others. On the 7th of August, Mr. Wheeler went before the Grand Jury. The result was an indictment for riot and assault and battery against these five persons, and also against Passmore Williamson, and William Still, the well-known clerk at the Anti-Slavery office. The case was called for hearing on the 9th inst., but the parties, not being ready for trial, showed cause for a continuance, which was granted.

On Wednesday morning, August 29th, they were all, excepting Passmore Williamson, put upon their trial, upon the charge of riot and assault and battery, in the Court of Quarter Sessions, in the city of Philadelphia, Judge Kelley presiding.

Wheeler appeared as the principal witness against the defendants: His testimony was substantially the same that he gave before Judge Kane. He swore that the "defendants came on board the boat, headed by Mr. Williamson; that Williamson, and the defendant, Still, talked to the woman Jane, and endeavored to persuade her to go off the boat; both Still and Williamson telling her that she was free and urging her to go ashore; she was asked by them if she did not wish to be free; she replied that she did, but *did not want to leave her master;* during the ringing of the last bell, *she was seized and carried down the gangway and on shore;* the two children were also seized and carried after her by the defendants."

On the cross-examination he said he did not remember whether he told her on the boat that she was free to go if she wished; but he declared that he "had said so before, had always felt so; did not want to have any one about him who did not wish to stay; had exercised no restraint or control over her; she knew perfectly well where she was going, and was satisfied to go."

Believing that all the persons who could contradict their testimony were included in the indictment, Wheeler and the other witnesses for the prosecution were emboldened to swear in the strongest manner to such points as they thought could not fail to secure a conviction. There amazement and confusion can be better conceived than described, when Jane Johnson suddenly appeared on the witness stand. Her testimony utterly destroyed that of Mr. Wheeler and his witnesses. It was as follows:

"I can't tell my exact age; I guess I am about 25; I was born in Washington City; lived there this New-Year's, if I shall live to see it, two years; I came to Philadelphia about two months ago.

I came with Col. Wheeler; I brought my two children, one aged 10, and the other a year or so younger; we went to Mr. Sully's and got something to eat; we then went to the wharf, then into the hotel.

Col. Wheeler told me to stay on the upper porch and did not let me go to dinner, and sent by the servants some dinner to me, but I did not desire any; after dinner he asked me if I had dinner; I told him I wanted none; while he was at dinner I saw a colored woman, and went to her and told her I was a slave woman traveling with a very curious gentleman, who did not want me to have anything to do or say to colored persons; she said she was sorry for me; I said nothing more; then I went back and took my seat where I had been ordered by Col. Wheeler; he had told me not to talk to colored persons; to tell everybody I was traveling with a minister going to Nicaragua; he seemed to think I might be led off; he did not tell me I could be free if I wanted to when I got to Philadelphia; on the boat he said he would give me my freedom; he never said so before; I had made preparations before leaving Washington to get my freedom in New York; I made a suit to disguise myself in—they had never seen me wear it—to escape in when I got to New York; Mr. Wheeler has that suit in his possession, in my trunk; I wasn't willing to come without my children; for I wanted to free them; I have been in Col. Wheeler's family nearly two years; he bought me from a gentleman of Richmond—a Mr. Crew; he was not a member of Col. Wheeler's family; Col. Wheeler was not more than half an hour at dinner; he came to look at me from the dinner-table, and found me where he had left me; I did not ask leave of absence at Bloodgood's Hotel; while Col. Wheeler went on board the boat a colored man asked me did I want to go with Col. W.; I told him "No, I do not;" at 9 o'clock that night he said he would touch the telegraph for me and some one would meet me at New York; I said I was obliged to him; no more was said then; I had never seen the man before; when Col. Wheeler took me on board he took me on the upper deck and sat us down alongside of him. While sitting there I saw a colored man and a white one; the white man beckoned me to come to him; the colored man asked did I desire my freedom; the white man approached Mr. W. and said he desired to tell me my rights; Mr. W. said, "My woman knows her rights;" they told me to go with them; he held out his hand but did not touch mine, and I immediately arose to go with him; I took my oldest boy by the hand; the youngest was picked up by some people and became very much alarmed, and I proceeded off the boat as quickly as I could, being perfectly willing and desirous to go; Mr. Wheeler tried to stop me, no one else; he tried to get before me as though he wanted to talk to me; I wanted to get off the boat, and didn't listen to what he had to say. I did not say I did not want my freedom; I have always wanted it; I did not say I wanted to go with my master; I went very willingly to the carriage, I was very glad to go; the little boy said he wanted to go to his massa, he was frightened; I did not say I wanted to go to Col. Wheeler; there was no outcry of any kind, my little boy made all the noise that was made."

The presentation of Jane as a witness, in the Court-room, was a bold and perilous act on the part of her friends, and one in which they would not have felt justified, had they not been assured that a strong force should be provided for her protection by the State authorities. Although they had this assurance, serious apprehensions were felt for the result. The United States officers were there with an extra force, evidently determined to arrest her. The officers of the Court and other State officers were there to protect the witness and vindicate the laws of the State. Vandyke, the United States District Attorney, swore he would take her. The State officers swore he should not, and for awhile it seemed that nothing could avert a bloody scene. It was expected that the conflict would take place outside of the door when she should leave the room, so that when she and her friends went out, and for some time after, the most intense anxiety pervaded the Court-Room. The way to the carriage was lined by a strong body of policemen, placed there by order of District Attorney Mann and Judge Kelley.

The courage of Vandyke and his allies seemed to pale before the stern determination of Judge Kelley and District Attorney Mann, to vindicate the dignity of the Courts and to enforce the laws of Pennsylvania, and Jane Johnson entered the carriage which was in waiting for her without disturbance. She was accompanied by an intrepid police officer, and the carriage was borne away in safety, and State sovereignty triumphed over the insolent invasion of usurped authority on the part of Federal officers.

Judge Kelley, in his charge to the Jury, a document honorable to
him as a man and as a judge, explicitly asserted "that when Col.
Wheeler and his servants crossed the border of Pennsylvania, Jane
Johnson and her two sons became as free as he."

The jury returned a verdict of "not guilty" as to all the parties
on the count charging them with riot. On the second count, charging
them with an assault upon Col. Wheeler, Ballard and Custis were
found "guilty"—the rest "not guilty." Ballard and Custis were
sentenced by Judge Kelley to pay a fine of ten dollars each and the
costs of prosecution, and to be imprisoned during one week. Measures
were taken to relieve these unfortunate men, who were doubtless
sufferers from perjury, of the pecuniary part of their burden. Thus
ended one act of this strange drama.

When Passmore Williamson was committed to prison, every
learned and upright lawyer, of our city, and every citizen capable
of appreciating and respecting the rights and true liberties of the
people under a free government, was shocked and alarmed by the
outrage upon the plainest principle of law and of justice, of
which Judge Kane had been guilty. But the people of Pennsylvania
never imagined that a sovereign State was impotent to redress the
wrong, and to protect against judicial error, folly, or wickedness, the
personal liberty of her own citizens. Their thoughts instantly and
naturally turned to the *habeas corpus;* that dear-bought right of a
free people, that sacred palladium of their liberty, in which our nation glories. To this Passmore Williamson might confidently ap-
peal. The aid of this he might demand, by undoubted right. He
did demand it. Application was made by his counsel to Chief Justice Lewis, of the Supreme Court of Pennsylvania, for a writ of *habeas corpus,* with a view to his liberation if the commitment of
Judge Kane should be found to be illegal. Judge Lewis, though
bound, by virtue of his office, to issue this writ upon such application, assumed the responsibility of refusing to do so, on the ground
that one Court should yield to another the respect which it claims for
its own adjudications!

Failing to obtain justice where it should have been promptly
awarded him, Mr. Williamson, by his counsel, renewed his application to the Supreme Court *in banc,* sitting at Bedford on the 13th
of August. His application was fully and ably argued by Messrs.
Charles Gilpin and Wm. M. Meredith. These gentlemen asserted
the petitioner's *right* to the writ, and earnestly protested against

being called upon to argue the question, in face of the imperative requisition of the act of 1785 ; that the writ shall be issued upon such petition, and its imposition of a penalty upon any judge who shall refuse to award it. Mr. Meredith concluded his eloquent and impressive argument with the following language :

"As regards the proceedings of the District Court, I have argued the question of jurisdiction only. The errors in law in other respects of these proceedings I shall not enter upon. The odd use of the writ of Habeas Corpus in applying it to the purpose of depriving a party of liberty, instead of restoring it ;—the allowing a traverse of the return, which can only be allowed by statute, and which no statute allows in the Courts of the United States—the taking that traverse by parol merely—the assuming to decide upon it the fact of abduction upon insufficient evidence, and from that to deduce a continuance of custody on no evidence at all— the absolute inconsistency of the record, which, after setting out a full, complete, and unevasive return, proceeds to a commitment for a supposed refusal to make any return,—I do not know that all these and other errors would of themselves enable this Court to interfere, if the District Court had jurisdiction of the case. But as the Court had no jurisdiction, these circumstances, all of them operating oppressively on a citizen entitled to your protection, do greatly aggravate the case, and enhance, if that be possible, your just obligation to relieve him. They do indeed tend to show a want of jurisdiction, for surely Providence would never have permitted a Court of competent jurisdiction to fall into so many errors in one case."   .   .   .   .   .

"I now leave the matter in the hands of the Court. It is impossible to conceal from ourselves the fact that the essential rights of this Commonwealth are invaded. This condition of things is inauspicious. To correct it, nothing is wanted but the firm and temperate discharge of your duties as magistrates and ministers of the law."   .   .   .

"The question here has nothing to do with the rights or wrongs, the conduct or misconduct of the North or the South. It concerns principles on which all are agreed. THAT EACH STATE HAS THE RIGHT TO REGULATE HER OWN DOMESTIC RELATIONS AND INSTITUTIONS—THAT THE COURTS OF THE UNITED STATES HAVE NO RIGHT TO INTERFERE WITH OR CONTROL THEM—THAT CITIZENS OF OTHER STATES THAT COME UPON HER SOIL ARE, WHILE THERE, BOUND TO RESPECT AND OBEY HER LAWS :—THESE, I say, are the principles involved here, and they are quite as dear to the SOUTH as to the NORTH : they ought to be quite as dear to the NORTH as to the SOUTH.

It has come to the point that, failing your aid, they are no longer safe in Pennsylvania.   I invoke that aid with confidence, and, if it be granted the rights of the Commonwealth will have been vindicated, and the affair from which these questions have originated—untoward in all its aspects—will be left to be determined by the laws of the State, in some appropriate forum."   .   .   .   .

Posterity will scarcely believe that Pennsylvania, boasting of her democracy, and her tenacious respect for State Rights, could have had a Supreme Bench of Judges, all of whom, *with one exception*, united in refusing to grant a writ of *habeas corpus* upon this application.   Yet such was the fact, and long will it be remembered, to the shame of the Commonwealth, and the disgrace of those judicial officers who perverted justice, and sought to establish iniquity by their interpretations of law.   Judge Black pronounced the opinion of the Court, which was concurred in by Judges Lewis, Woodward and Lowrie.   The writ was refused for the following reason, expressed in the language of Judge Black :

" We have no authority, jurisdiction or power to decide anything here except the simple fact that the District Court had power to punish for contempt a person who disobeys its process—that the petitioner is convicted of such contempt—and that the conviction is conclusive upon us. The jurisdiction of the Court on the case which had been before it and everything which preceded the conviction are out of our reach, and they are not examinable by us—and, of course, not now intended to be decided."

Thus it has been determined, by the highest judicial authority of Pennsylvania, that the etiquette of courts towards each other, is of greater value, and its maintenance of more importance, than the dearest rights and the personal liberties of the citizens. However unworthy or illegally a Federal Judge may imprison any man or woman of this commonwealth, though his decision may be the result of stupid ignorance, personal dislike, or desire for revenge, (and the world's history furnishes abundant proof that judges may be guilty of all these,) there is no redress for the outraged citizen ; the officers of the State, who were appointed by the people to protect him against such outrage deliberately connive with his persecutor, and even the right of a free people to the *habeas corpus is sacrificed to the etiquette of Courts !*

The Court, in this case of Passmore Williamson, not only denied to him that which was his by legal right, but, it stooped to insult a prisoner with taunts worthy of the judicial bench of England in the days of James the Second. Incapable of comprehending the moral heroism which suffers imprisonment and death, for the sake of a *principle*, these judges sneeringly intimate that he is covetous of the honors of martyrdom ; and, then, with the heartless sarcasm of an Inquisitor over his tortured victim, they coolly tell him that he " carries the key of his prison in his own pocket," and " can come out when he will, by making terms with the Court that sent him there." The terms which he must make, are, of course, the disavowal of what he believes to be truth, and the utterance of what he believes to be a lie, and *they* cannot imagine why he does not make them ; the key which would open his prison door, is the stain of perjury on his soul, and they cannot imagine why he does not use it.

From this decision, which will be remembered, with that of Judge Kane, long after the authors of both will wish them forgotten, Judge Knox emphatically and earnestly dissented. He closes his very ably written opinion, in dissent, with the following recapitulation of the grounds on which he would have awarded the writ.

"1. At common law, and by our statute of 1785, the writ of habeas corpus ad subjiciendum is a writ of right, demandable whenever a petition in due form asserts what, if true, would entitle the party to relief.

2. That an allegation in a petition that the petitioner is restrained of his liberty by an order of a Judge or Court without jurisdiction, shows such probable cause as to leave it no longer discretionary with the Court or Judge to whom application is made whether the writ shall or shall not issue.

3. That where a person is imprisoned by an order of a Judge of the District Court of the United States for refusing to answer a writ of habeas corpus, he is entitled to be discharged from such imprisonment if the Judge of the District Court had no authority to issue the writ.

4. That the power to issue writs of habeas corpus by the Judges of the Federal Courts is a mere auxiliary power, and that no such writ can be issued by such Judges where the cause of complaint to be remedied by it is beyond their jurisdiction.

5. That the Courts of the Federal Government are Courts of limited jurisdiction, derived from the Constitution of the United States and the acts of Congress under the Constitution, and that when the jurisdiction is not given by the Constitution or by Congress in pursuance of the Constitution, it does not exist.

6. That when it does not appear by the record that the Court had jurisdiction in a proceeding under our habeas corpus act to relieve from an

illegal imprisonment, want of jurisdiction may be shown by proving the facts in the case.

7. That where the inquiry as to the jurisdiction of a Court arises upon a rule for a habeas corpus, all the facts set forth in the petition tending to show want of jurisdiction are to be considered as true, unless they contradict the records.

8. That when the owner of a slave voluntarily brings his slave from a slave to a free State, without any intention of remaining therein, the right of the slave to his freedom depends upon the law of the State into which he is thus brought.

9. That if a slave so brought into a free State escapes from the custody of his master while in said State, the right of the master to reclaim him is not a question arising under the Constitution of the United States or the laws thereof; and therefore a Judge of the United States cannot issue a writ of habeas corpus directed to one who it is alleged withholds the possession of the slave from the master, commanding him to produce the body of the slave before said judge.

10. That the District Court of the United States for the Eastern District of Pennsylvania has no jurisdiction because a controversy is between citizens of different States, and that a proceeding by habeas corpus is in no legal sense a controversy between private parties.

11. That the power of the several Courts of the United States to inflict summary punishment for contempt of Court in disobeying a writ of the Court is expressly confined to cases of disobedience to lawful writs.

12. That where it appears from the record that the conviction was for disobeying a writ of habeas corpus, which writ the Court have no jurisdiction to issue, the conviction is *coram non judice,* and void.

For these reasons I do most respectfully, but most earnestly, dissent from the judgment of the majority of my brethren refusing the writ applied for."

All honor should be rendered to Judge Knox, for his fidelity to law and the right, in opposition to all his fellow-judges. The people will remember him.

Subsequently to the announcement of the decision of the Court, and the dissenting opinion of Judge Knox, Judge Lowrie published his opinion, wherein he differs, on some points, from the decision. He says :

" I have a very strong impression that no Court is justified in issuing a *habeas corpus* for the purpose of restoring a slave to his master; and that is very plainly the purpose for which the writ was issued out of the District Court. I do not think that our writ has any such purpose, or ever had. It was intended to secure the liberty of the subject, and not to try rights of property."

*   *   *   *   *   *   *   *

"I have, moreover, a very strong impression that there is no way in which the case before the District Judge can be regarded, that would entitle the Federal Judiciary to take cognizance of it."

He proceeds to say that he had been willing to grant the writ and hear the case; but after this expression of opinion, he enters upon an argument against the interference of one Court with another, and concludes by concurring in the refusal of the writ. It does not appear what were the reasons and motives which operated in changing his opinion during the interval between the sittings of the Court in Bedford and in Philadelphia, but, more grossly inconsistent than his fellow-judges, in spite of his "very strong impression" that the prisoner is illegally and unjustly imprisoned by a judge who had no jurisdiction in the case, he deliberately refuses to perform his judicial duty in redressing the wrong!

Citizens of Pennsylvania! what shall be the end of these things? An officer of the Federal Government has usurped authority in a case wholly beyond his jurisdiction, and without law, or the shadow of law, has immured in one of your prisons, a citizen of Pennsylvania. Your own Supreme Bench of Judges fold their hands, and refuse to enforce your laws for his protection. In the person of Passmore Williamson, the rights of every man and woman of this commonwealth have been invaded, and you now hold your possession of personal liberty, and its defense, the *habeas corpus*, in which you have gloried, at the mercy of judicial tyrants who may, at any hour, summon you into their presence, by illegally issued writs of *habeas corpus*, and, on charges of constructive contempt, commit you to prison without bail, and without hope of redress. Will you take warning before it is too late, and arouse yourselves to defend your liberties, and avert the evil which threatens every citizen of this State? Lord Camden, who has been styled, "one of the purest Judges who ever adorned the English Bench," has said: "*The discretion of a judge is the law of tyrants. It is always unknown. It is different in different men. It is casual, and depends upon constitution, temper, and feeling. In the best, it is oftentimes caprice; in the worst, it is every vice, folly and passion, to which human nature is liable.*"

The Slave power of this nation, which has been long and steadily encroaching upon the rights of the North, emboldened by success, has evidently resolved to re-establish slavery on your soil, by asserting and maintaining, in defiance of your laws, the right to carry and hold their slaves wherever they choose to go, under the Constitution of the United States. In this insolent attempt it seems to have found an assistant in one of your own citizens, who, from his seat in the District Court of the United States, defies and tramples on the laws of Pennsylvania, and perverts "the great remedial process by which *liberty is vindicated and restored*," to the base purpose of reducing free persons to slavery. John H. Wheeler attempted to carry off, as slaves, from Pennsylvania, persons whom your laws declare to be free, and by so doing rendered himself liable to the legal penalties which you have affixed to the crime of kidnapping. Judge Kane asserts that "he who unites with others to commit a crime, shares with them all the legal liabilities that attend on its commission."— Out of his own mouth and by your laws is he condemned.

If you will tamely submit to these outrages on your laws and on your rights, what can you expect but that the usurped power which has stricken down the habeas corpus, in Pennsylvania, will rob you of the trial by jury, and of the freedom of speech and the press, when it shall serve its purpose so to do. The bold wickedness which dared the one, will be capable of the other. Lay not the flattering unction to your souls that this case concerns the interests of one individual only; it involves the honor and safety of every citizen of the commonwealth. While Passmore Williamson is thus imprisoned, the sovereignty of the State and the true liberty of her citizens lie prostrate in the dust. On you rests the solemn responsibility of choosing whether your dearest rights shall hang upon the caprice of a tyrant, or whether you will assert the sovereignty of the State, and teach these law-defying Judges to tremble before the indignation of a justly incensed people.

Since the foregoing narrative has been prepared for the press, another Decision has been pronounced by Judge Kane, in the District Court of the United States. It was in reply to a petition of Jane Johnson, presented by her counsel, J. B. Townsend and John M. Read, Esqrs., showing that she is one of the three parties named in the writ of Habeas Corpus issued in the case of John H. Wheeler *versus* Passmore Williamson, and stating *First*, that Wheeler had no control over her or her children at the time of issuing the aforesaid writ, they then being free; *Second*, that the writ was issued against her wish; *Third*, that since she left Mr. Wheeler, which, she asserts, she did of her own will and desire, she has not been restrained of her liberty by Mr. Williamson, or any other person; and *Fourth*, that under this writ of habeas corpus, a writ designed to restore freemen to liberty when unduly restrained thereof, John H. Wheeler seeks to recover the petitioner and her children, and reduce them again into slavery. She therefore prays that the writ may be quashed, and that Passmore Williamson may be discharged from his imprisonment.

Judge Kane refused the application to enter this paper among the records of the Court, on the ground that Jane Johnson had no *status* in the Court. A very small part of the decision relates directly to the application before the Judge, the principal portion of it being an elaborate defense of his conduct towards Passmore Williamson. The most important point of his decision is the bold assertion of the right of the slaveholders to pass, *with their slaves*, through Pennsylvania or any other State of the Union. He asserts this on the ground that slaves are *property*, and asks, " How can it be that a State may single out this one kind of property from among all the rest, and deny to it the right of passing over its soil—passing with its owner, parcel of his travelling equipment, as much so as the horse he rides on, his great coat, or his carpet-bag ?" The decision is a bold revelation of what a discerning eye could see from the beginning of this case, that the object and determination was and is, to obtain possession of Jane Johnson and her children and re-enslave them, and to this base end he is keeping, and is determined to keep, Passmore Williamson in prison.

Notwithstanding the well-established fact that it is and was utterly beyond the power of Mr. Williamson to bring Jane and her children before the Court; that neither she nor her friends would suffer him to expose her to such peril, even *if he had wished to do so*, Judge Kane says:

" His duty, then as now, was and is, to bring in the bodies, or, if they had passed beyond his control, to declare, under oath or affirmation, so far as he knew, what had become of them." [That is, to give the information which will enable the claimant either to recover his property, or to hold some one else for their value.] " And from this duty, or from the constraint that seeks to enforce it, there can be no escape."

Pennsylvanians are now to decide whether they will submit to the establishment of slavery on their own soil; whether they will permit slaves to be carried or *driven* across their State singly or chained in coffles, or whether they will enforce *their own laws* for the protection of freedom. If this right of transit be granted, who is to decide how long a time slaveholders, or slavedrivers with their gangs, may spend in " passing through " a free State, or what operations peculiar to their trade, though revolting to humanity, they may be permitted to engage in. Judge Kane's defense of his persecution of Passmore Williamson, on the ground that Pennsylvania may be made a slaveholding State, whenever a trafficker in human beings chooses to drive his victims through it, will not avail for his justification before the tribunal of the PEOPLE.

LETTER FROM PASSMORE WILLIAMSON.

The following letter was written by Passmore Williamson in reply to one addressed to him by a gentleman of New York city, inquiring respecting further legal means for his relief. The only just grounds on which he could obtain redress having been set forth in his petition to the Supreme Court of Pennsylvania, and that Court having declined to act in the case, Mr. Williamson has exhausted the means of legal redress provided by the State, and he indignantly rejects the other alternative of dishonorable submission to the tyranny of usurped power.

"No. 78 PHILADELPHIA COUNTY PRISON, }
Sept. 29, 1855. }

DEAR SIR : Your letter of the 27th inst. is now before me, and in reply to your inquiry, I may say that I contemplate no further legal proceedings with reference to my liberation from this jail, in which I am now confined. I have now been kept here for more than two months, and I can see no prospect of liberation. I am a native, and have always been a citizen of Pennsylvania ; and believing myself atrociously wronged, I applied to the highest tribunal known to our laws, but relief has been withheld. I can expect none from the authority that placed me here, without dishonorable submission. Having been guilty neither of falsehood, dissimulation, nor contumacy, I am sure that it is no case for a degrading capitulation. Such a course would bring with it a diminution of self respect more oppressive than the power now seeking to crush out the highest attribute of State sovereignty by immuring me within these walls

Accept for yourself, and communicate to others who favor me with their consideration, my most grateful acknowledgements.

Respectfully yours, &c.,
P. WILLIAMSON."

At the PHILADELPHIA ANTI-SLAVERY OFFICE, No. 31 North Fifth St., Anti-Slavery Books, Tracts and Newspapers may be always obtained ; and a free Reading Room is open to the public.